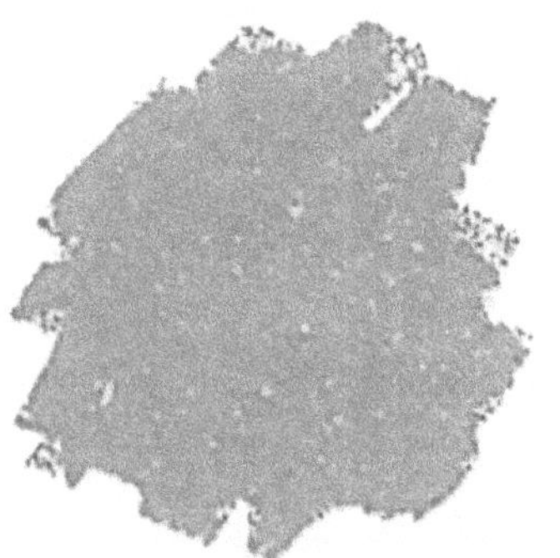

Red

Yellow

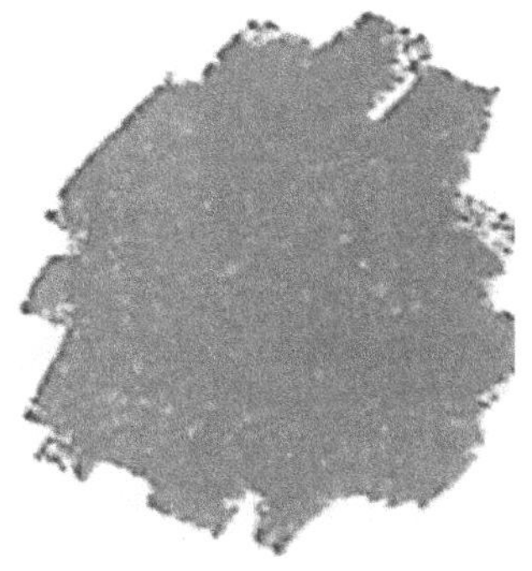

Blue

Secondary Colours

Orange

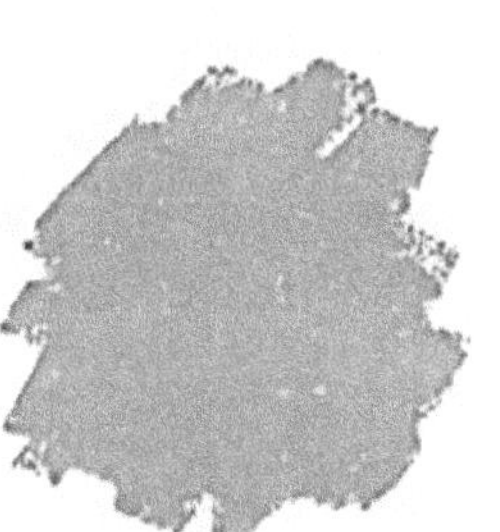

Green

Deep Yellow

Purple

Pink

Sky Blue

Grey

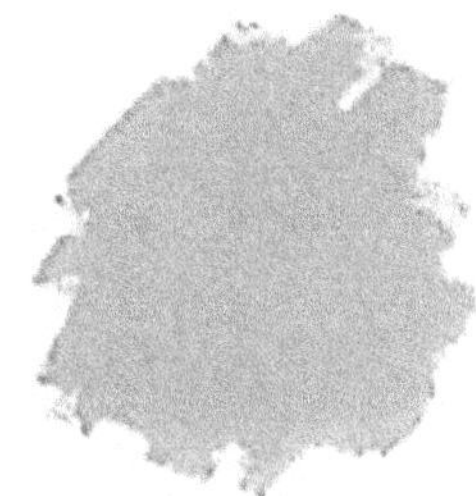

Parrot Gree

TRACE THE LINES

TRACE THE LINES

Remarks

Excellent | Good | Fair

Teacher's Signature: _______________

Date: _____ – _____ – 20 _____

TRACE THE LINES

 Colour the square.

 Trace and colour the square.

Remarks

○ Excellent   ○ Good   ○ Fair

Teacher's Signature: _______________

Date: ____ – ____ – 20 ____

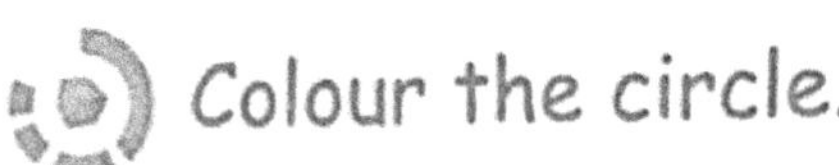 Colour the circle.

 Trace and colour the circle.

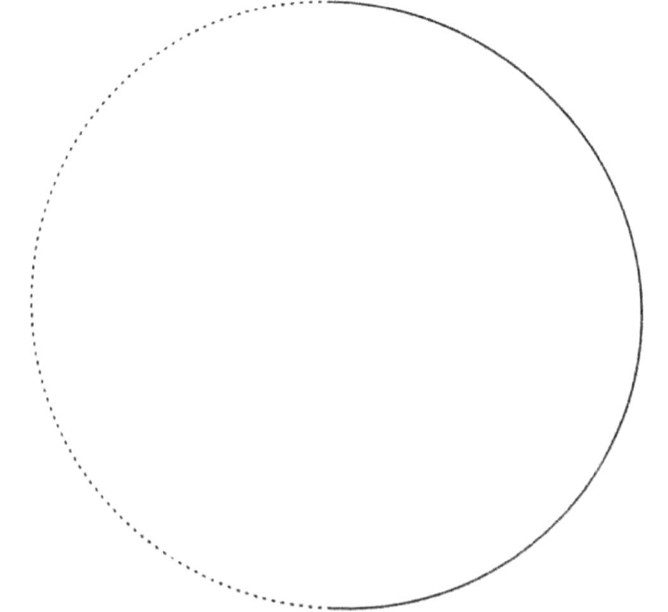

Remarks

◯ Excellent   ◯ Good   ◯ Fair

Teacher's Signature: _______________

Date: _____ – _____ – 20 _____

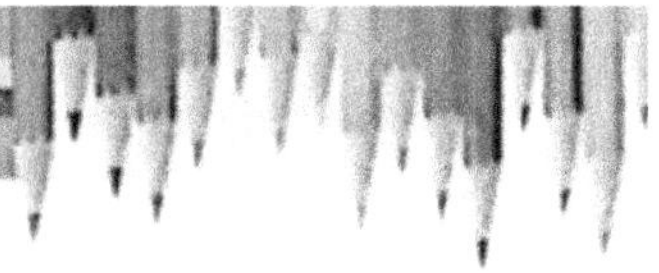

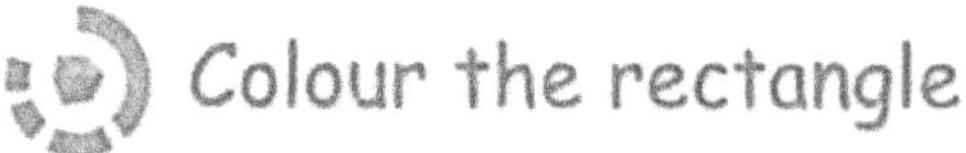 Colour the rectangle.

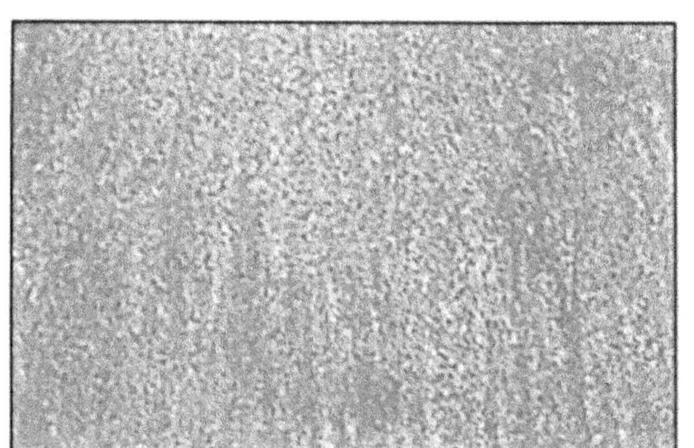

Trace and colour the rectangle.

 Colour the triangle.

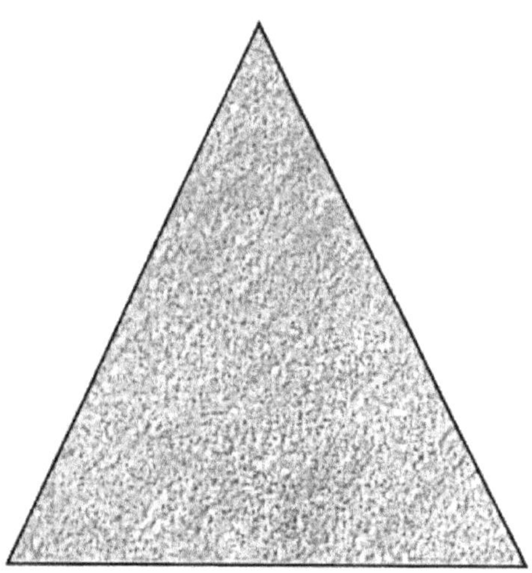

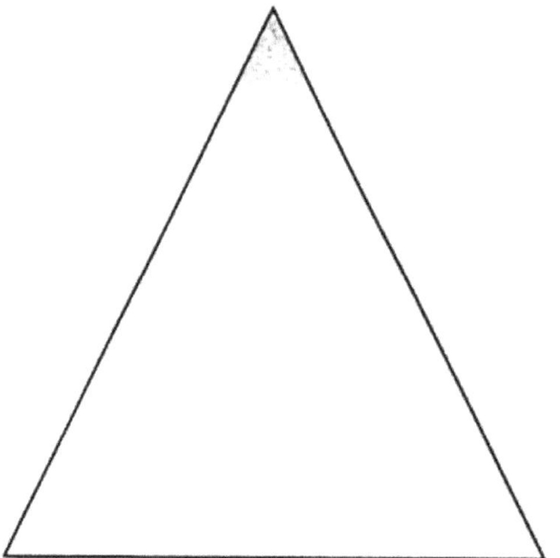

 Trace and colour the triangle.

Remarks			
⬤ Excellent	○ Good	○ Fair	

Teacher's Signature: ___________________

Date: _____ – _____ – 20 _____

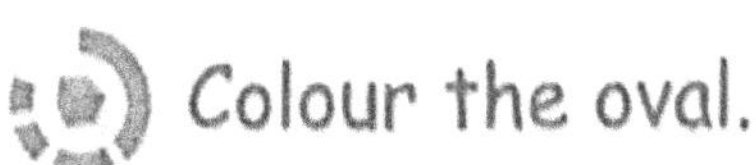 Colour the oval.

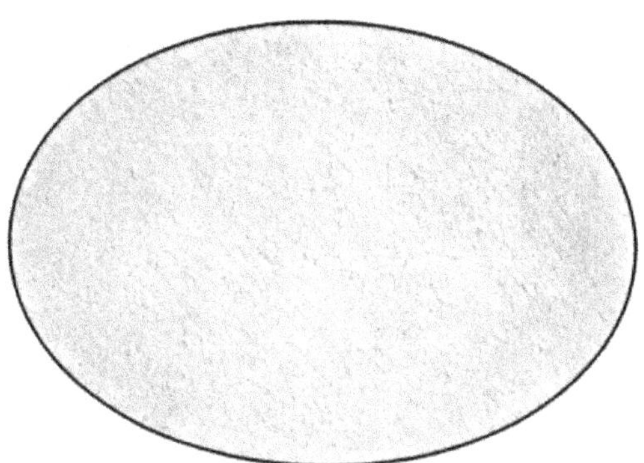

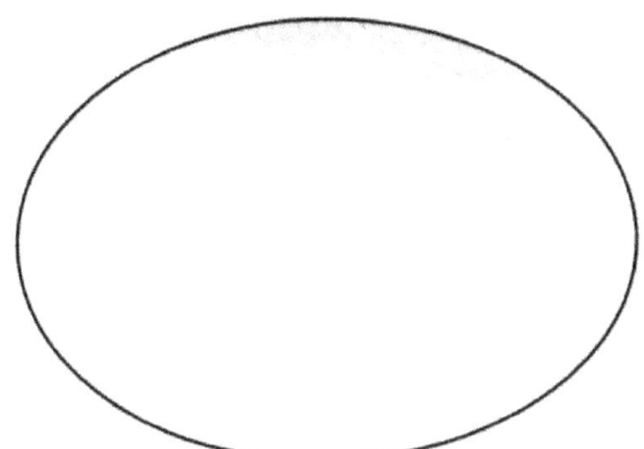

 Trace and colour the oval.

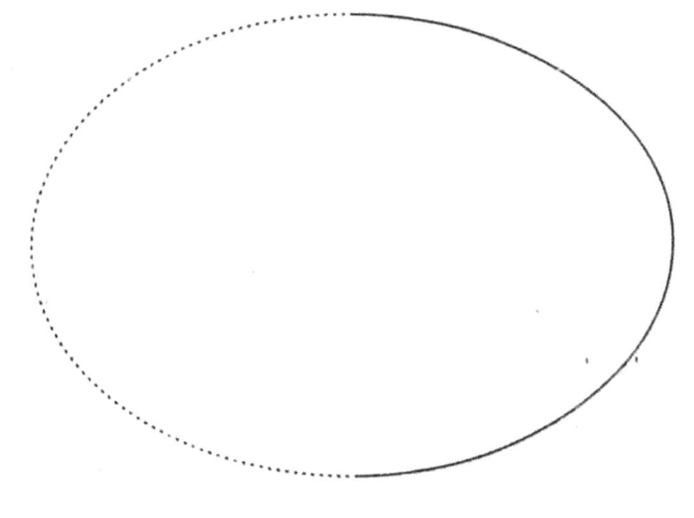

Remarks

○ Excellent | ○ Good | ○ Fair

Teacher's Signature: _______________

Date: ____ – ____ – 20 ____

ACTIVITY

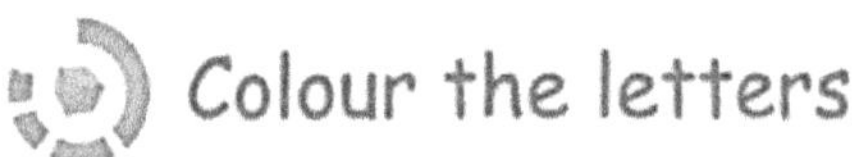 Colour the letters.

A B C D E F

A B C

D E F

Teacher's Signature: ______________

Date: ____ – ____ –20 ____

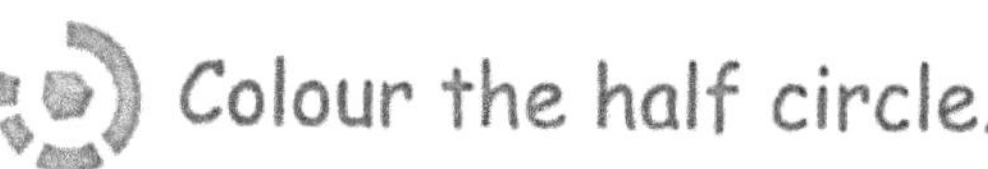 Colour the half circle.

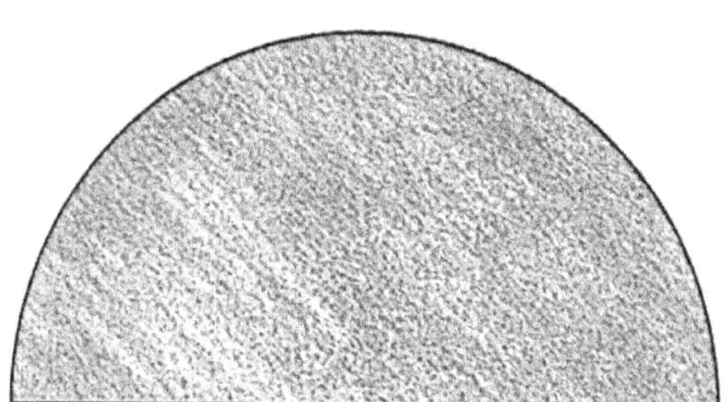 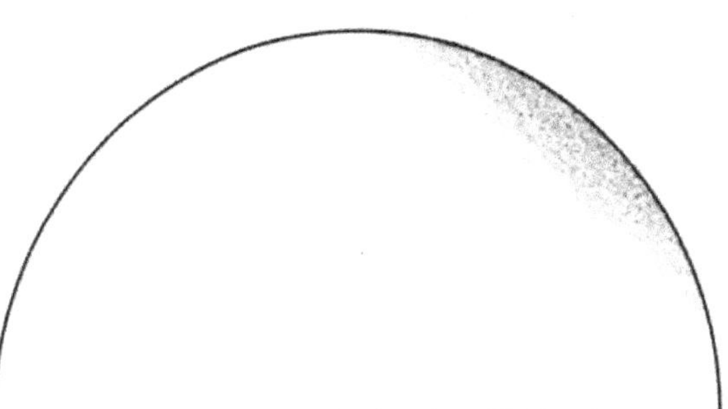

 Trace and colour the half circle.

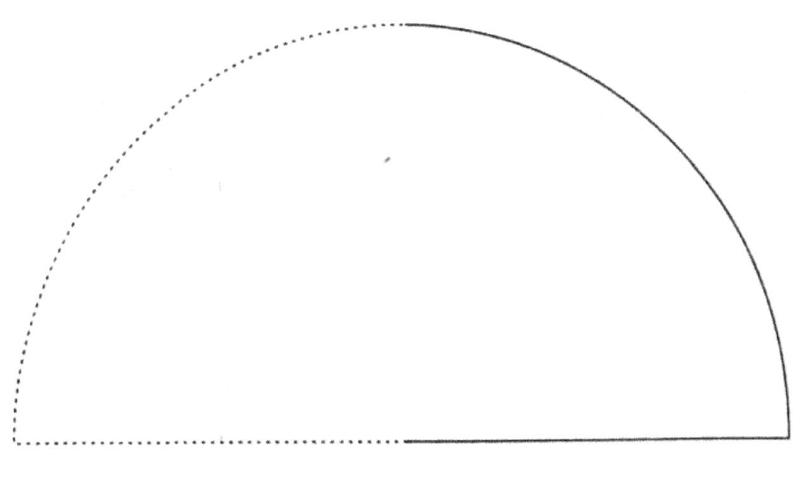

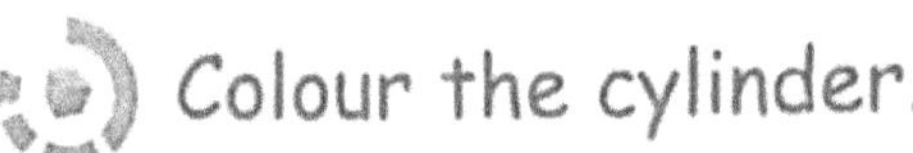 Colour the cylinder.

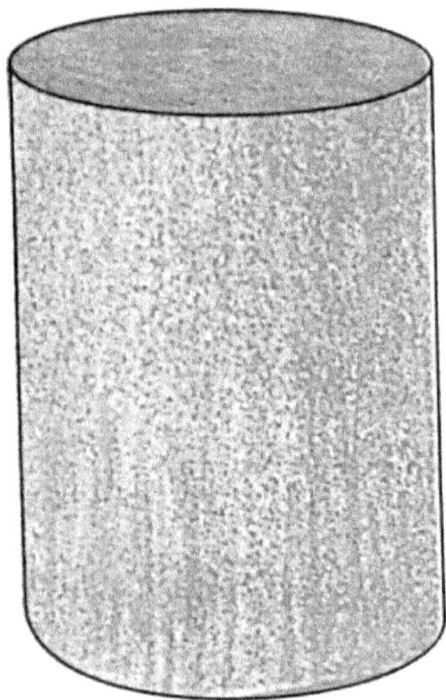 

 Trace and colour the cylinder.

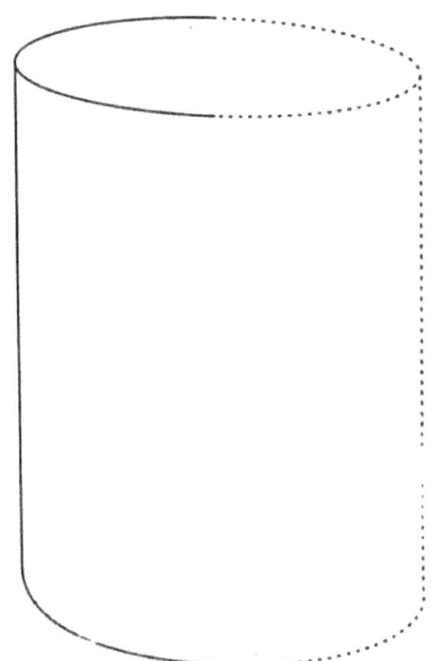

 Colour the cube.

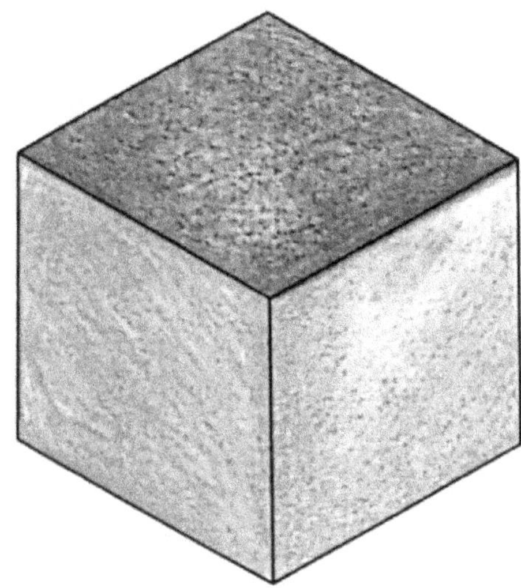

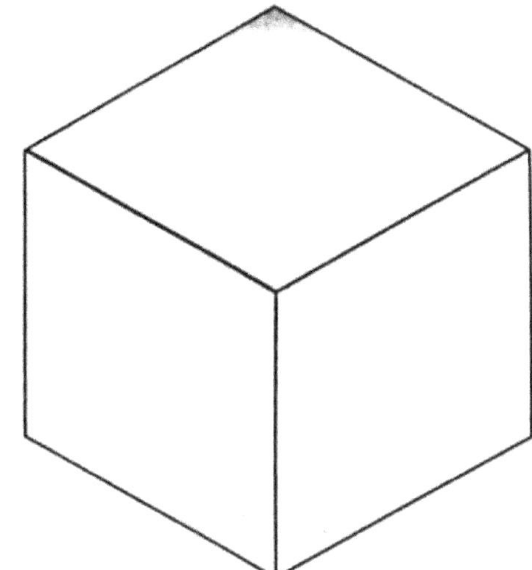

 Trace and colour the cube.

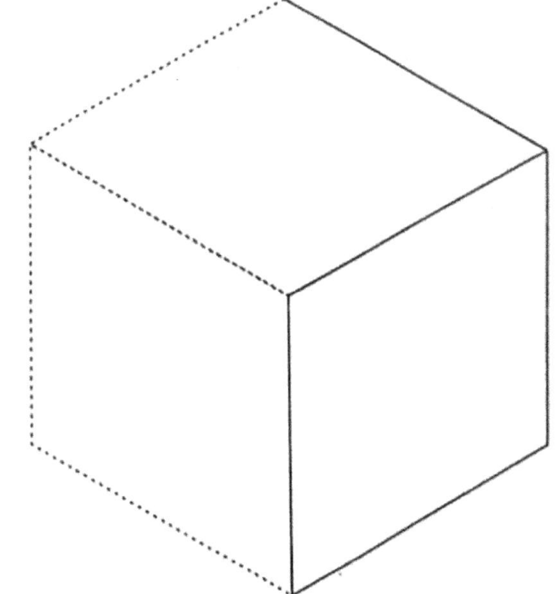

 Colour the star.

 Trace and colour the star.

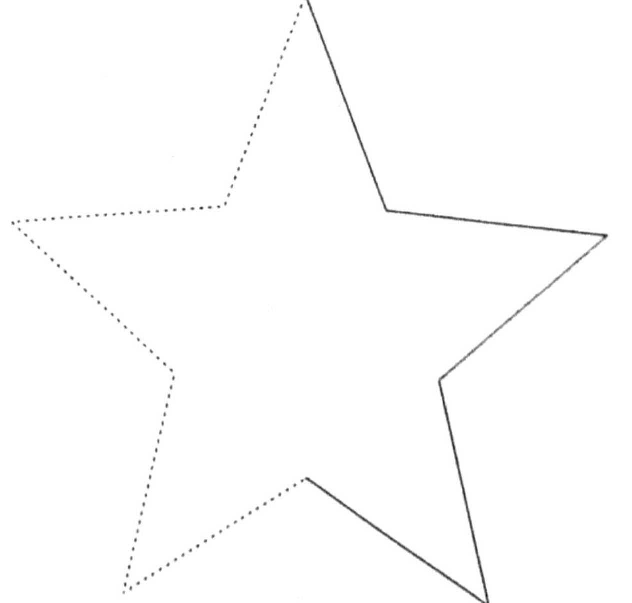

ACTIVITY

Colour the shapes.

Remarks

Excellent | Good | Fair

Teacher's Signature: __________

Date: ___ – ___ –20

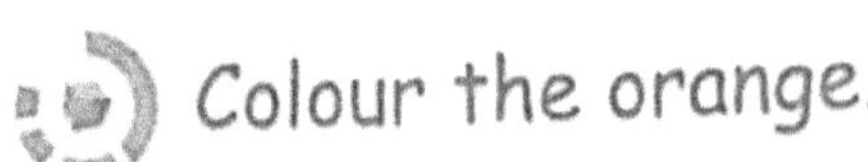 Colour the orange.

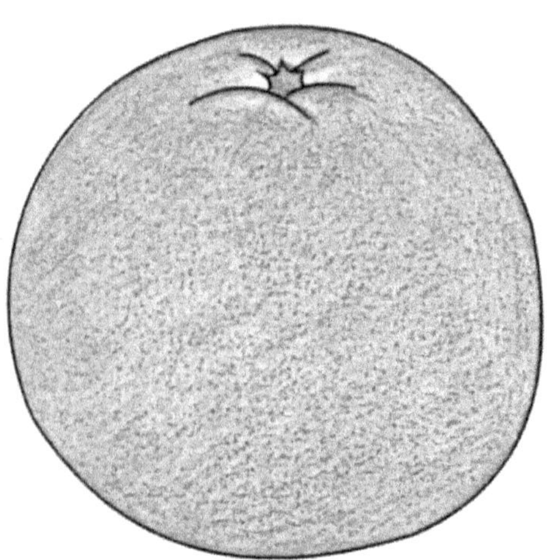 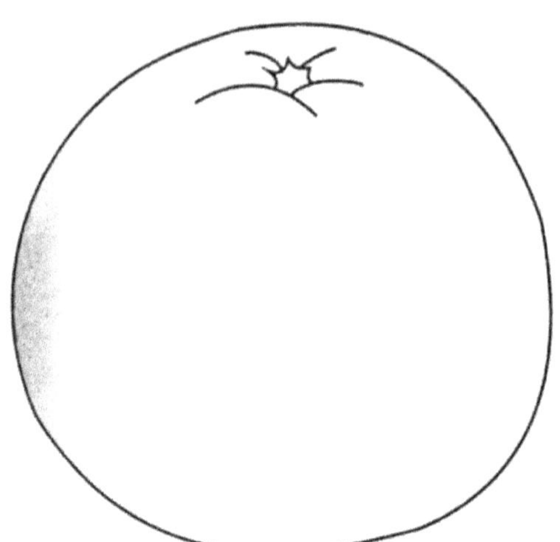

 Trace and colour the orange.

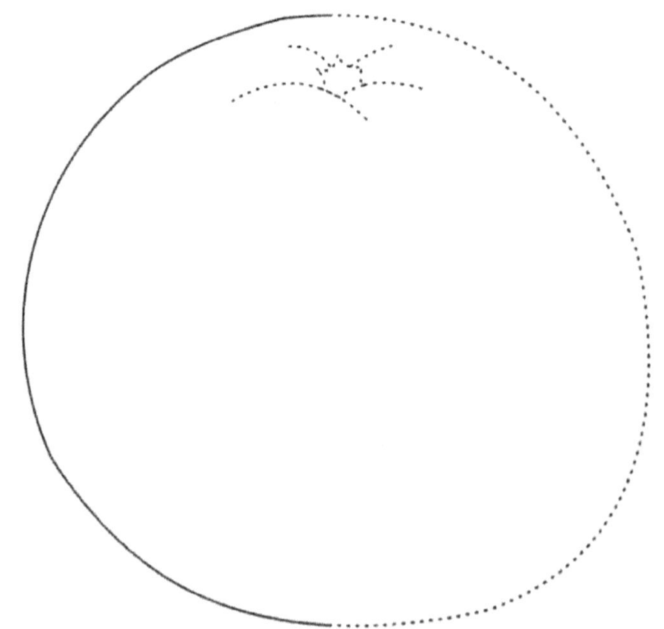

 Colour the glass.

 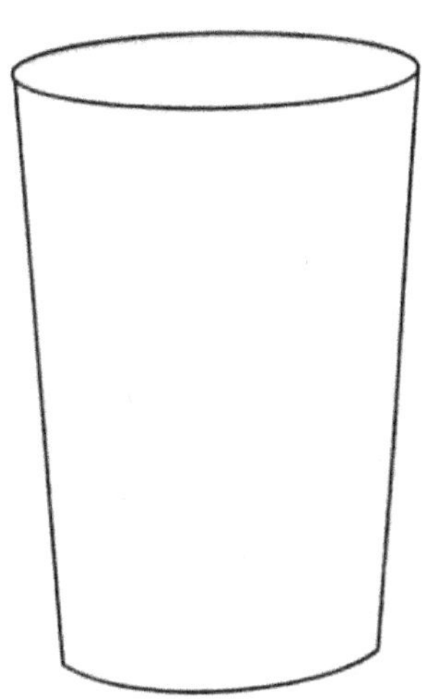

 Trace and colour the glass.

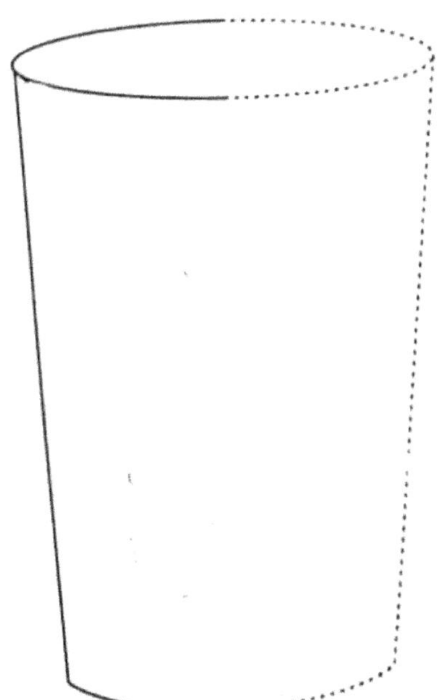

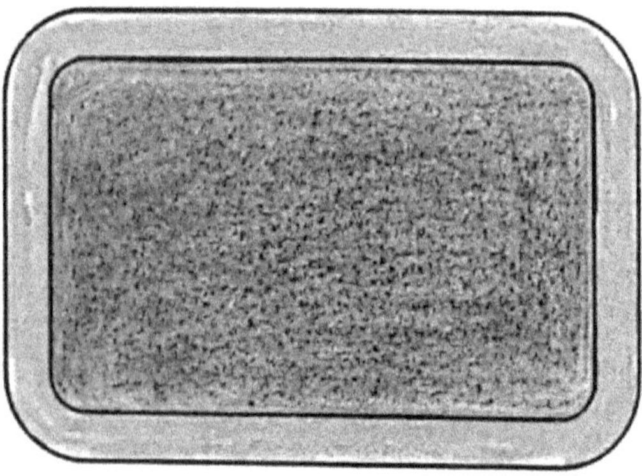 Colour the slate.

 Trace and colour the slate.

Remarks
○ Excellent | ○ Good | ○ Fair

Teacher's Signature: __________

Date:_____ - ____ - 20

 Colour the apple.

 Trace and colour the apple.

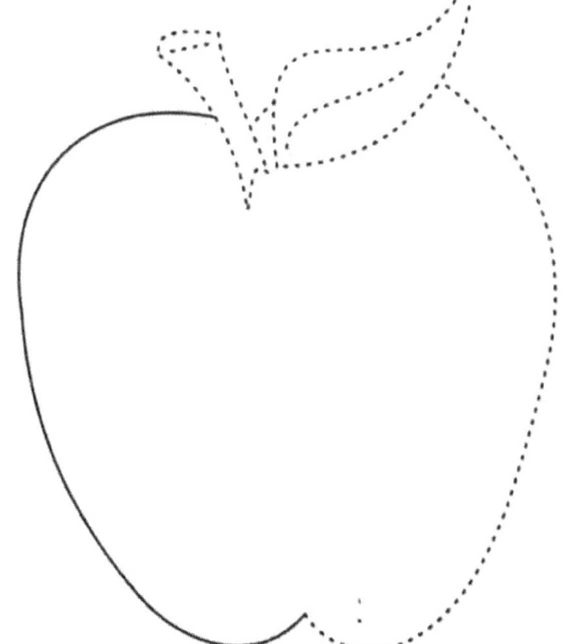

Remarks

○ Excellent ○ Good ○ Fair

Teacher's Signature: _______________

Date: ____ – ____ – 20

 Colour the tablet.

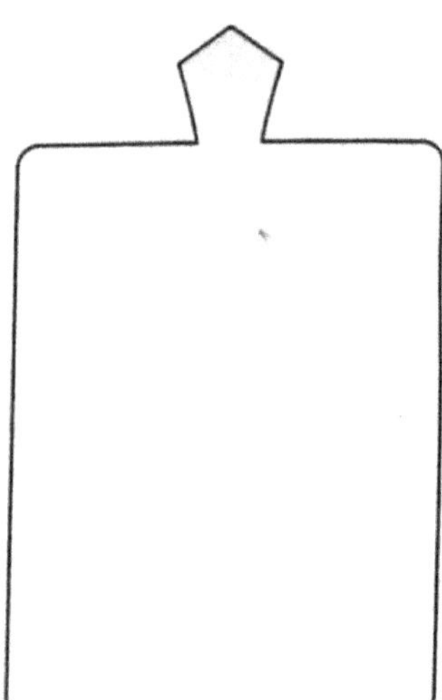

 Trace and colour the tablet.

Remarks

◯ Excellent | ◯ Good | ◯ Fair

Teacher's Signature: _______________

Date: ______ – ______ – 20 ______

ACTIVITY

Colour the numbers 1 to 8.

Remarks

⬤ Excellent   ◯ Good   ◯ Fair

Teacher's Signature: _______________

Date: ____ – ____ – 20 ____

 Colour the egg.

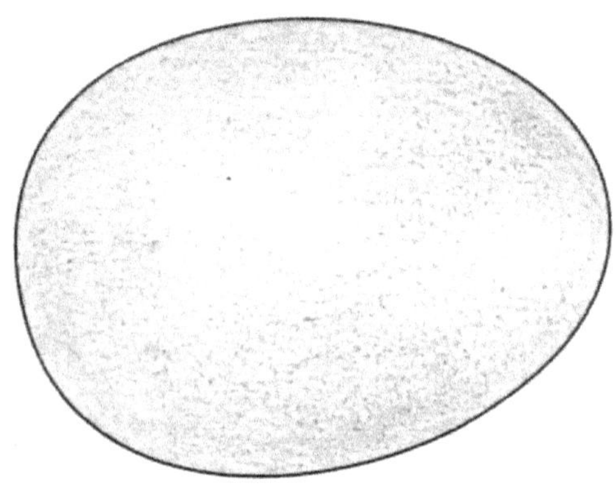

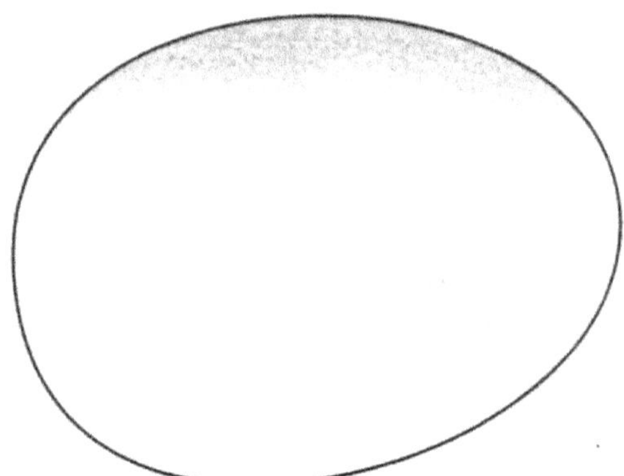

Trace and colour the egg.

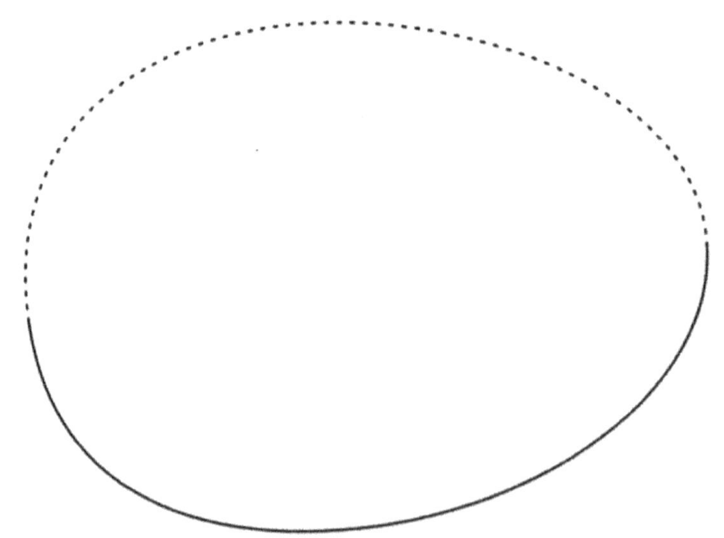

 Colour the pear.

 Trace and colour the pear.

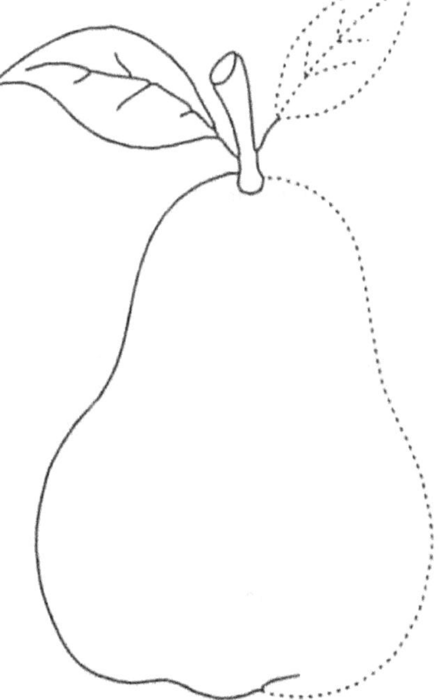

Teacher's Signature: ___________

Date: _____ – _____ – 20

 Colour the pizza.

Trace and colour the pizza.

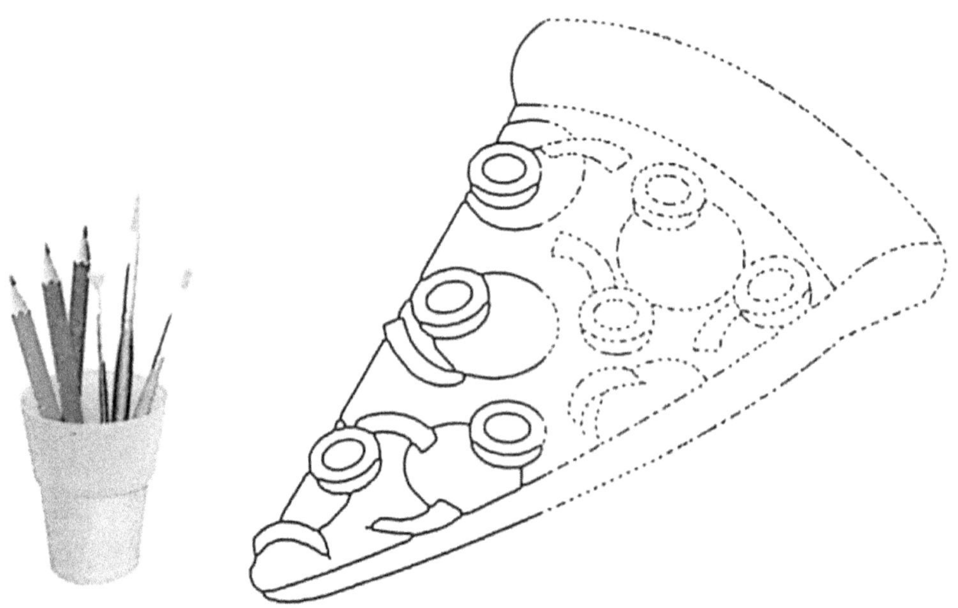

 Colour the pomegranate.

Trace and colour the pomegranate.

Remarks

◯ Excellent | ◯ Good | ◯ Fair

Teacher's Signature: _______________

Date: ______ – ______ – 20 _______

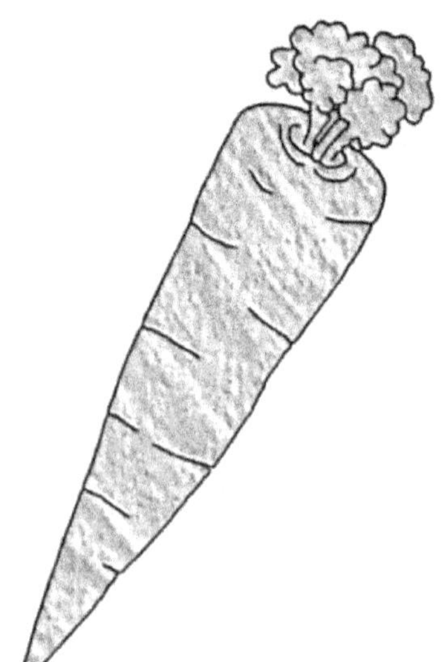 Colour the carrot

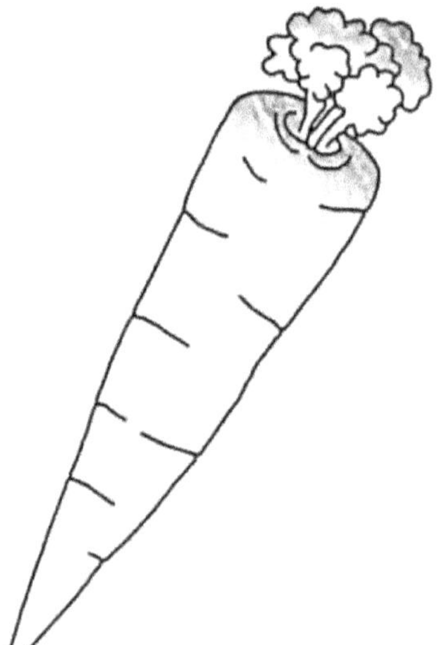

Trace and colour the carrot.

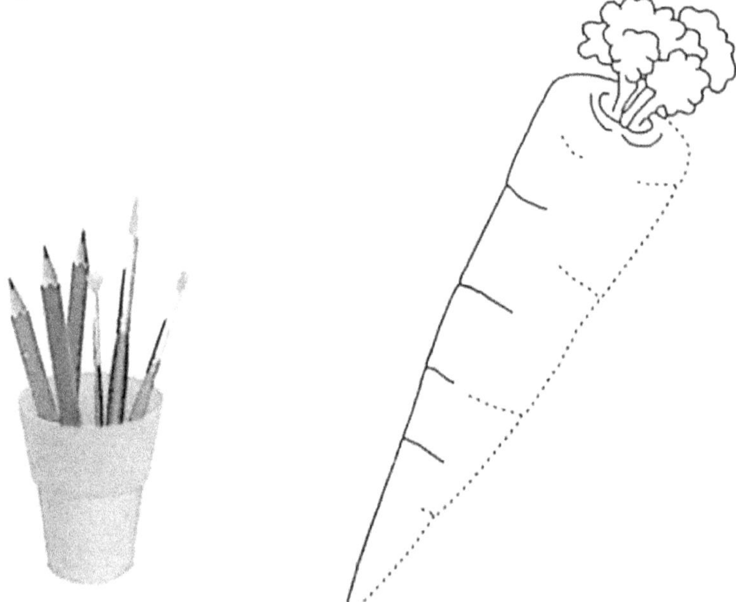

 Colour the mango.

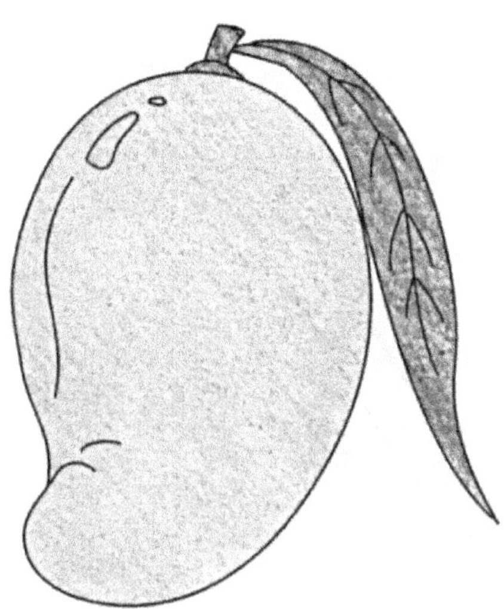
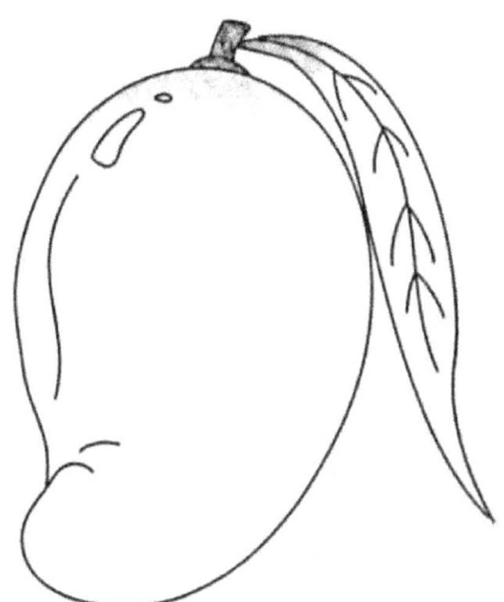

Trace and colour the mango.

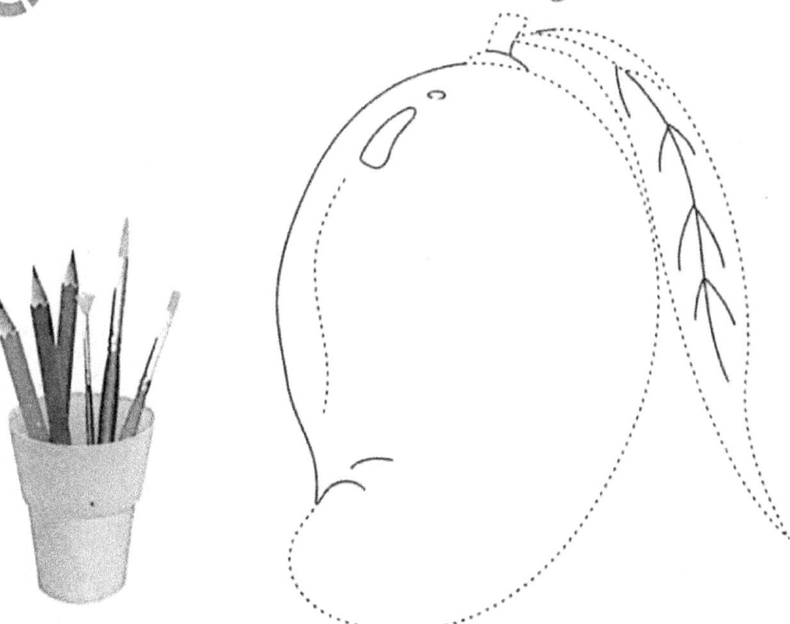

Teacher's Signature: _______________

Date:_____ – _____ – 20 _____

 Colour the bat.

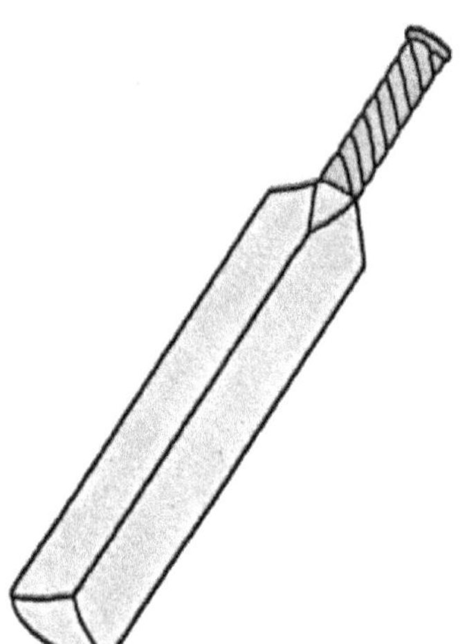 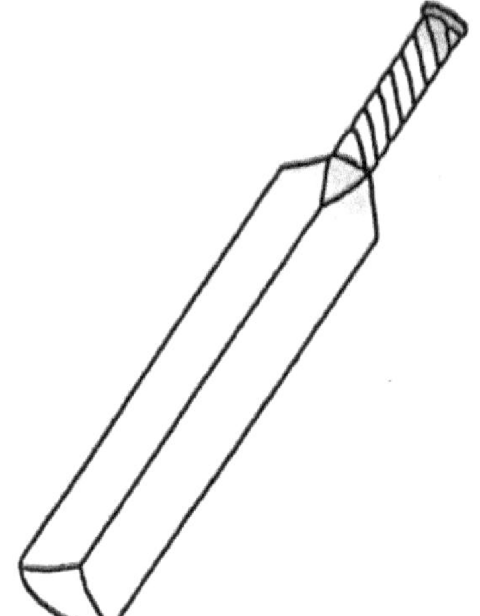

 Trace and colour the bat.

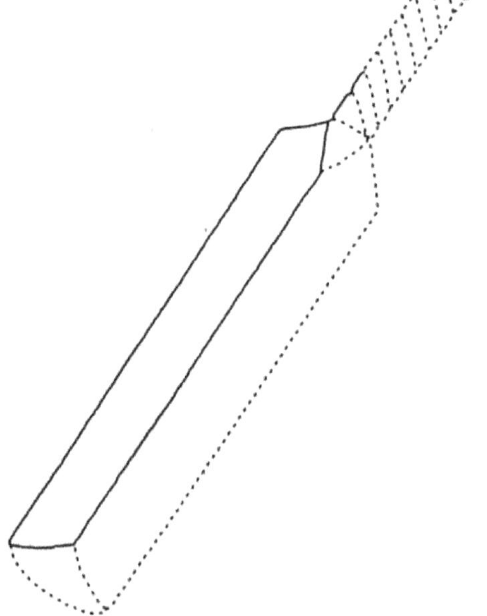

ACTIVITY

Trace and colour the star yellow, pomegranate red, pear green and glass blue.

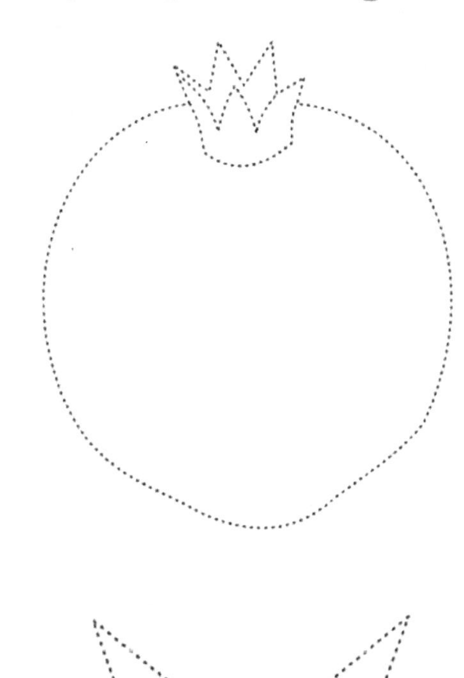

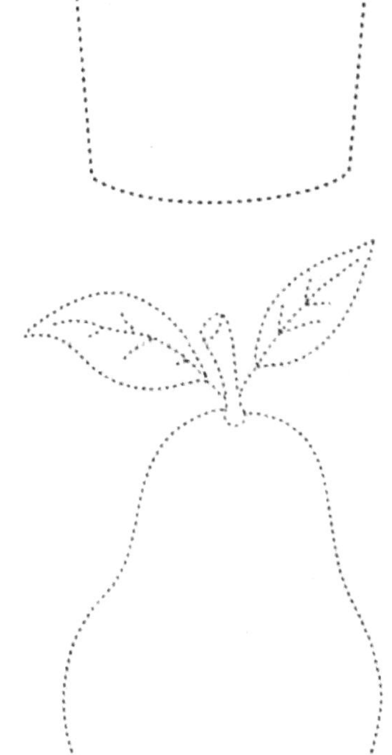

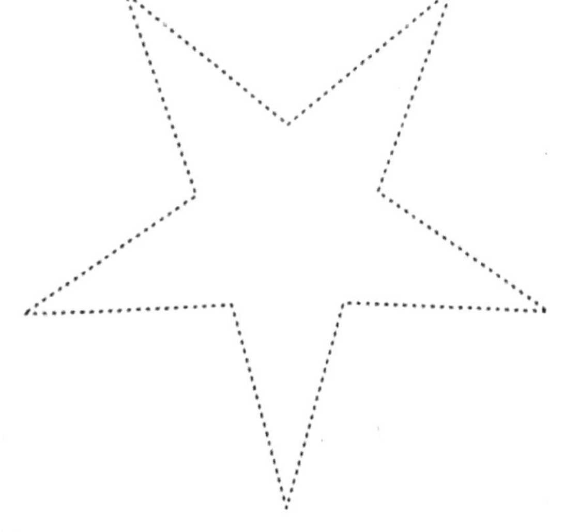

Teacher's Signature: ___________

Date: ___ ___ -20

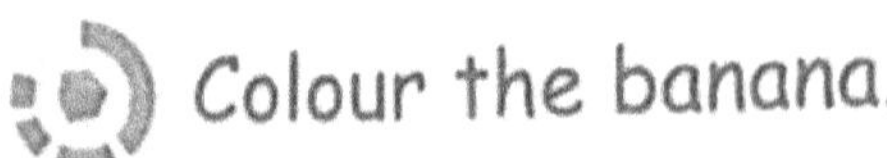 Colour the banana.

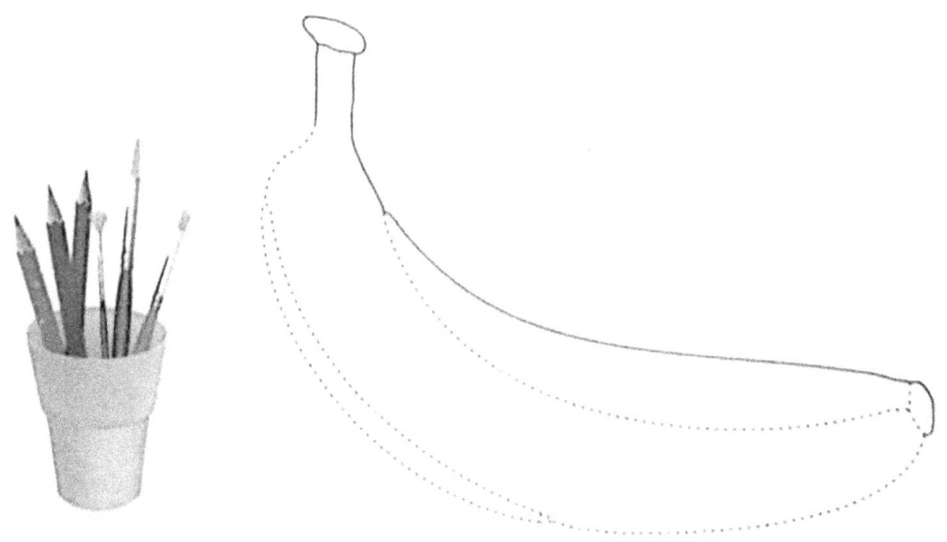 Trace and colour the banana.

Colour the cap.

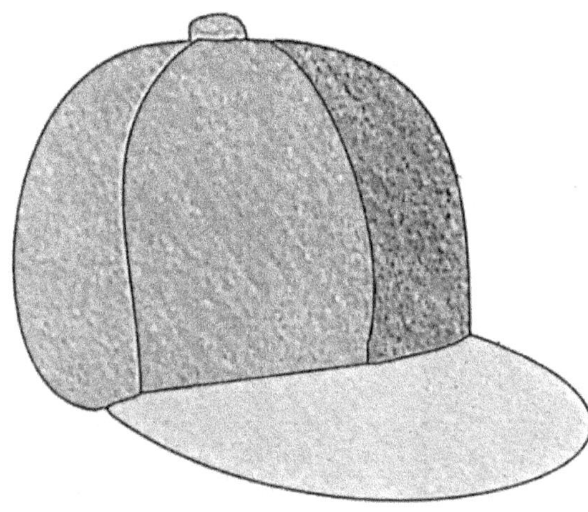

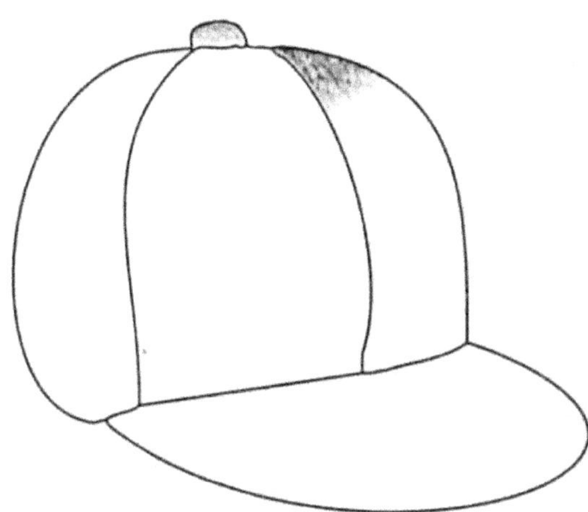

Trace and colour the cap.

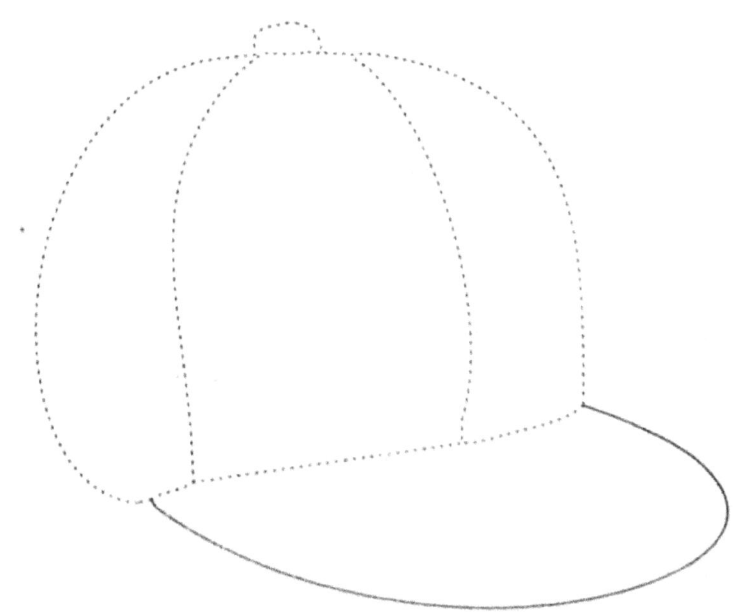

Remarks
Excellent | Good | Fair
Teacher's Signature: _______________
Date: ___ − ___ − 20 _______

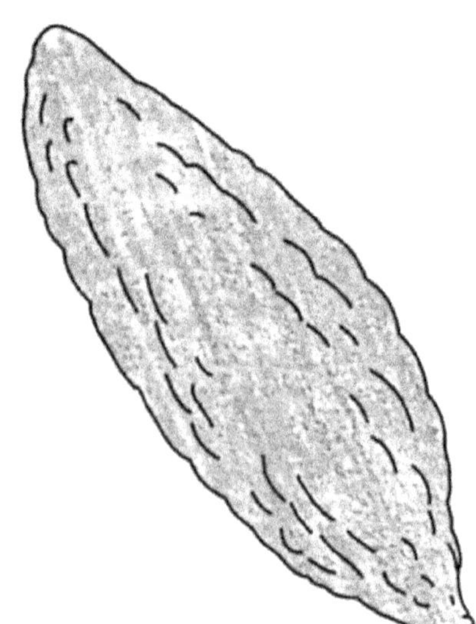 Colour the bitter gourd.

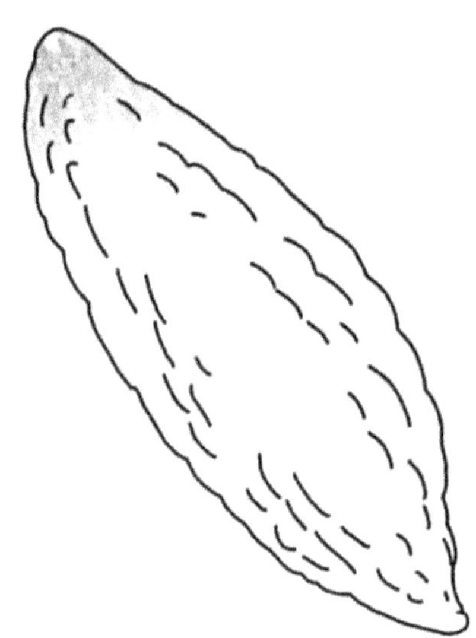

Trace and colour the bitter gourd.

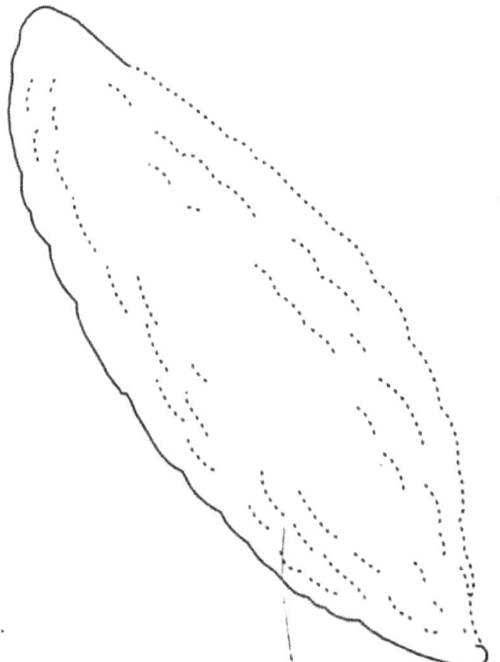

Remarks

◯ Excellent ◯ Good ◯ Fair

Teacher's Signature: ___________

Date: ____ – ____ – 20 ____

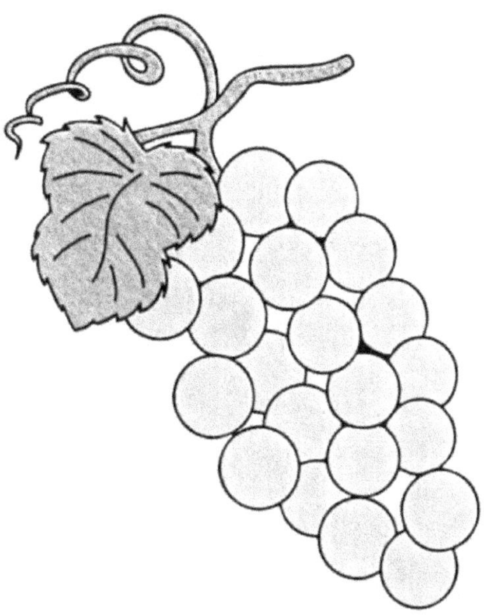 

Excellent | Good | Fair

Teacher's Signature: _______________

Date: ____ - ____ - 20 ____

 Colour the balloon.

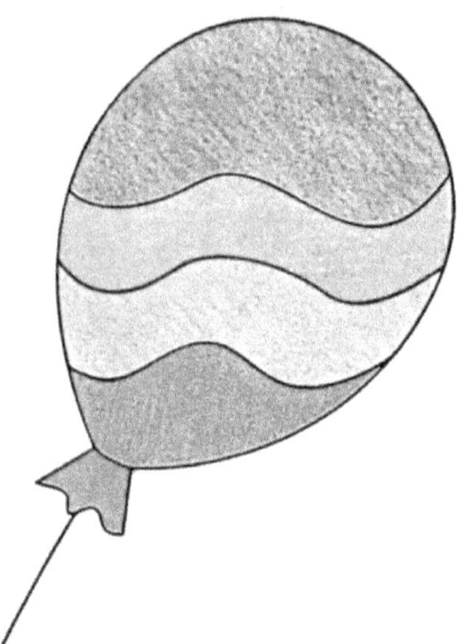

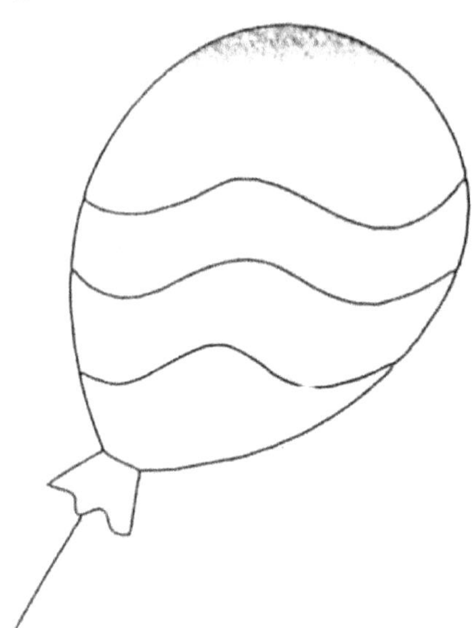

Trace and colour the balloon.

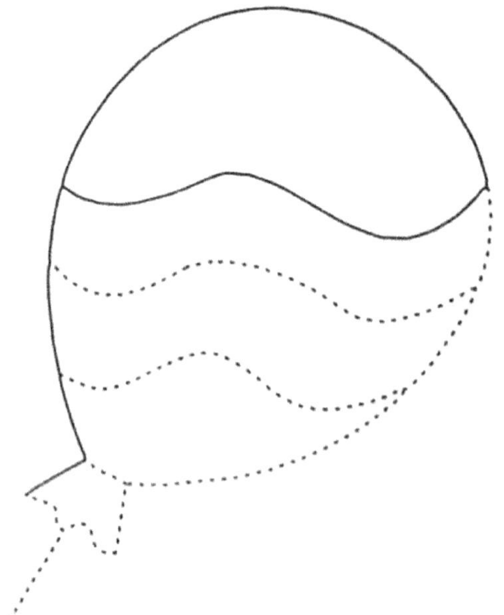

Remarks

◯ Excellent | ◯ Good | ◯ Fair

Teacher's Signature: _______________

Date: _____ – _____ – 20

Cut and Paste

Cut the objects and paste on the page # 39.

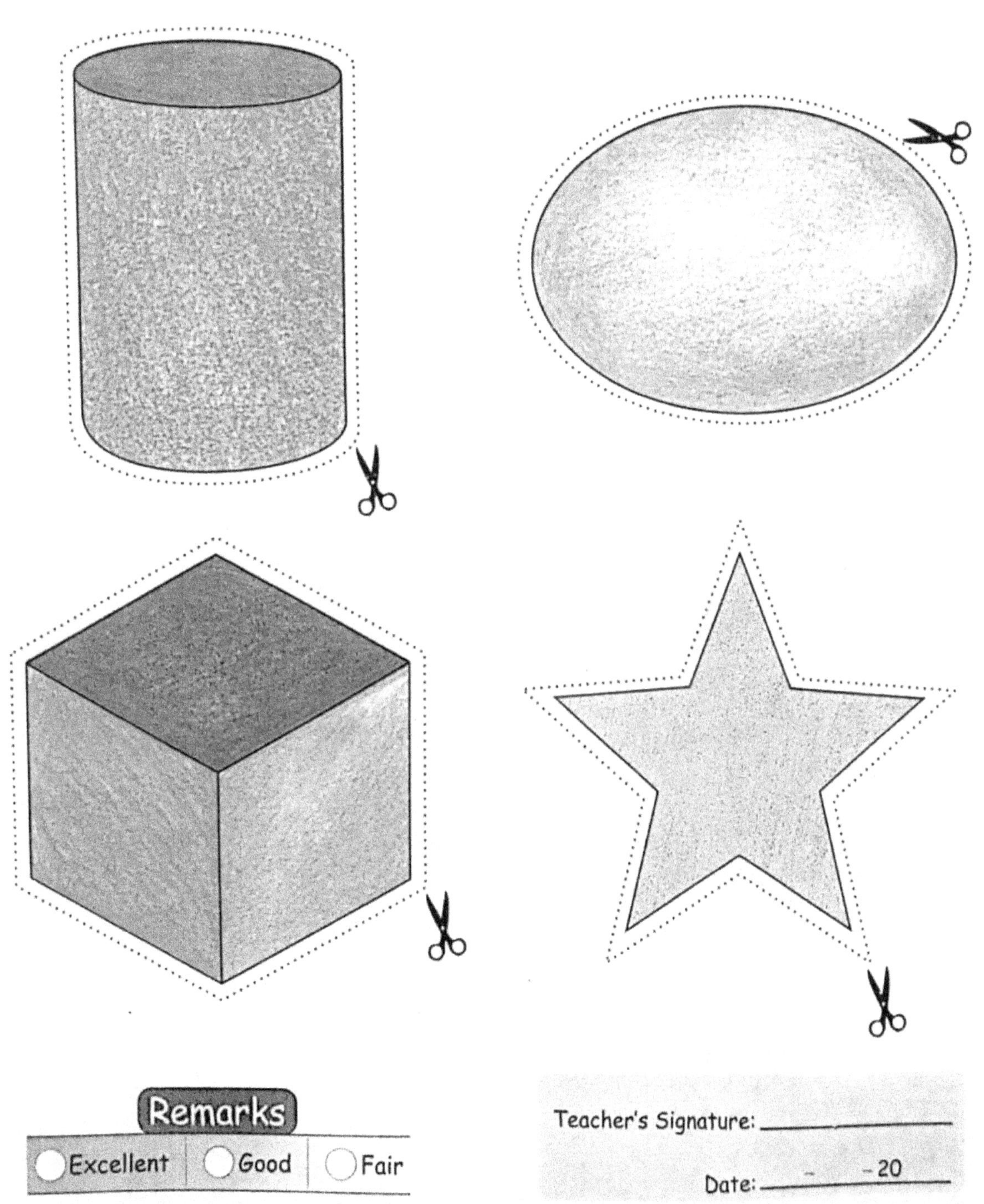

 Paste the cutting objects here.

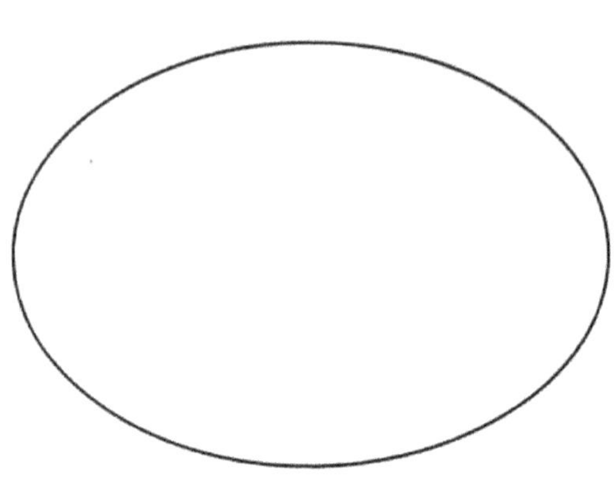

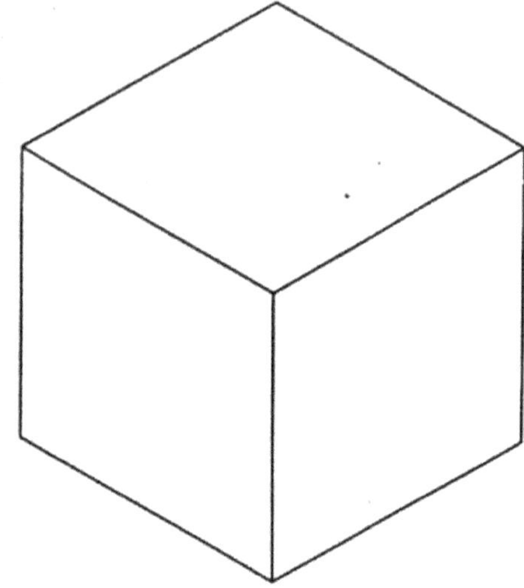

ACTIVITY

 Colour the fruit and basket.

www.ingramcontent.com/pod-product-compliance
Lightning Source LLC
Chambersburg PA
CBHW081405160726
48000CB00010B/3482